THE BACKUP PLAN
ICE MY PHONE KIT

Written By

JANET GREENWALD
&
LAURA GREENWALD

Published by Get Your Stuff Together
Productions Lion and The Rock Entertainment

LION AND THE ROCK
ENTERTAINMENT

For information about special discounts and bulk purchases go to www.getyourstufftogether.com or email us at corporatesales@getyoustufftogether.com.

Manufactured in the United States of America

ISBN: 978-1508420200

Table Of Contents

FOREWORD

In 2005, when I created the ICE, In Case of Emergency concept and campaign little did I know ICE would become a global phenomenon and still running just as strong more than a decade later.

Little did I realise then also was that my incredibly simple idea would take me on travels far and wide, meeting other like-minded individuals who also shared my aspirations.

When Laura and Janet Greenwald entered my life, it quickly became evident this entrepreneurial team were not satisfied with merely helping others prepare for the unexpected; they were and are passionate about a much wider holistic approach. After all, if we can make the unexpected any less unpleasant or devastating for ourselves and our loved ones, why stop there?

In providing a comprehensive portfolio of emergency preparedness material for all, Laura and Janet are empowering each of us; whichever method we choose to utilise for making a difference to outcomes we just cannot see coming.

As a paramedic, my shifts were littered with those I attended and who were conscious stating *"I didn't think I'd be in this position today when I woke."*

Remember, none of us 'likes' to be harbingers of doom but the reality is in considering a plan, we can more easily forget about the possibilities, safe in the knowledge we are in at least some way, prepared.

Bob Brotchie
Award Winning Founder of ICE, Former UK Paramedic
www.incaseofemergency.org

Before You Begin

Before You Begin

In each section of this book, you'll not only learn how to put an ICE Contact on every type of smart and cell phone, but you'll also learn how to do other things like make emergency wallet cards or create a medical information form.

To make it even easier, they come with downloadable forms that you can print and fill out by hand or complete right on your computer.

So before we get started, go ahead and download the materials that come with this book at this link http://getyourstufftogether.com/download/ICEMyPhoneKit.zip.

How To Download a ZIP file

To download a zip file, right click on the link, choose "Save Target As", and save the Zip file to your desktop. If you would rather, you can also download and save each document one by one. For more information go to:
http://getyourstufftogether.com/download/downloadingdocuments.pdf

How To Open a ZIP File
A ZIP file is a little folder that holds all of your documents zipped up inside for easy downloading. Once you download it, you'll see a little icon that looks like a file box. Double click on it, it will open and all the files will appear.

You can extract the documents one of two ways: 1) Click the extract button and all of the files will be extracted from the box and land on your desktop. 2) Highlight all the files, click CTRL +C to copy them and then CTRL+V to paste them onto your desktop.

How to Get a Copy of Adobe's Free Adobe Reader PDF Software
Go to www.adobe.com and follow the instructions to download the latest free PDF software from their website.

How To ICE Contacts On Your Cell Phones

The Two Minute ICE Contact

Learning how to put an ICE Contact on your phone is probably the main reason you purchased this book.

But as we all know, as much as we know we *should* do something, sometimes it doesn't seem like there are enough hours in the day to do it. As much as we try to squeeze everything in, it doesn't always happen.

That's why we created the Two Minute ICE Contact. It's a basic contact that will do nicely, until you have the time to do a detailed one, which will take about ten minutes. You'll find instructions for a full contact for your particular phone later in the book. But for now, here is a way to get a basic ICE Contact on your iPhone or Samsung Galaxy in two minutes.

What is A Two Minute ICE Contact?

During Hurricane Katrina, so many people were injured & separated from their families, that emergency workers came up with the idea of putting an ICE – In Case Of Emergency – contact in their cell phones. Now, hospitals worldwide, check patient's phones for their ICE contact, to locate their next of kin.

Problem is, an ICE Contact can take five or ten minutes to put into your iPhone. Not a lot of time, but when you're in between tasks and want to get it done while you're thinking about it – something we definitely suggest – five or ten minutes can be longer than you really have time for.

Not to worry. That's why we created the two minute version. Everything thing you absolutely need to have in your contact, until you have a few extra minutes to turn your quickie ICE Contact into a real lifesaver.

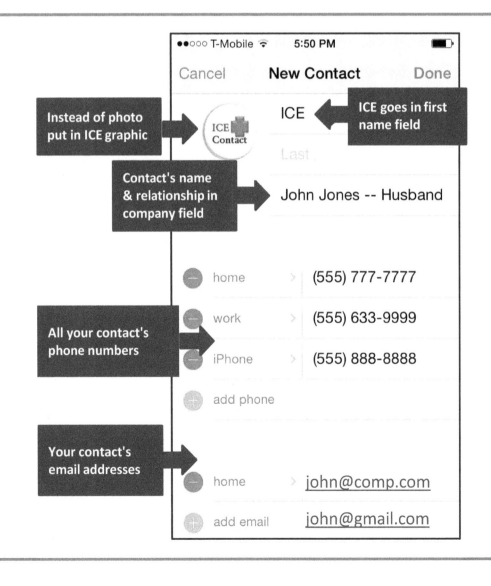

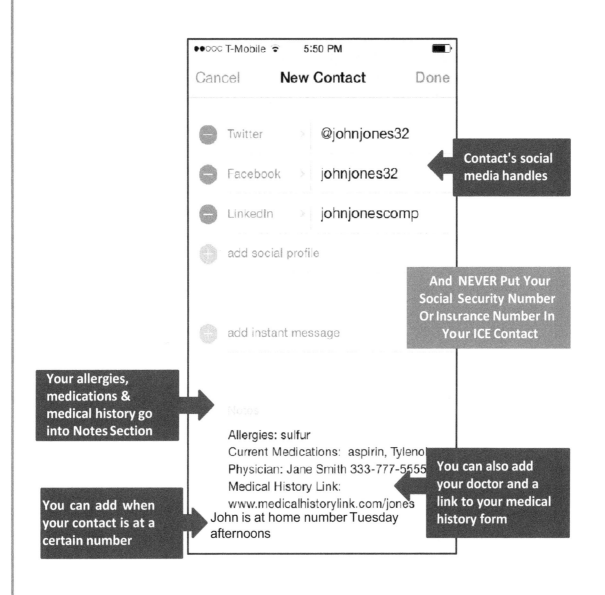

What is A Two Minute ICE Contact?

During Hurricane Katrina, so many people were injured & separated from their families, that emergency workers came up with the idea of putting an ICE – In Case Of Emergency – contact in their cell phones. Now, hospitals worldwide, check patient's phones for their ICE contact, to locate their next of kin.

Problem is, an ICE Contact can take five or ten minutes to put into your iPhone. Not a lot of time, but when you're in between tasks and want to get it done while you're thinking about it – something we definitely suggest – five or ten minutes can be longer than you really have time for.

Not to worry. That's why we created the two minute version. Everything thing you absolutely need to have in your contact, until you have a few extra minutes to turn your quickie ICE Contact into a real lifesaver.

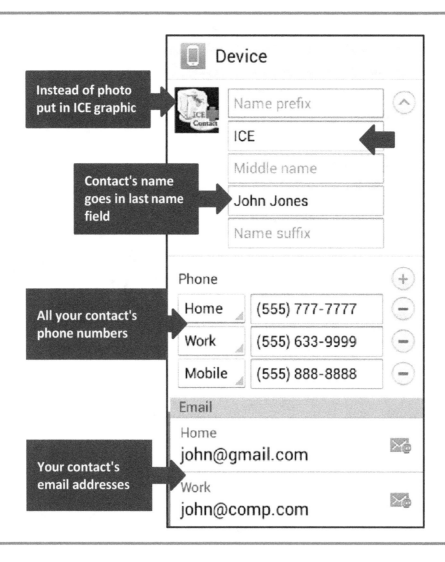

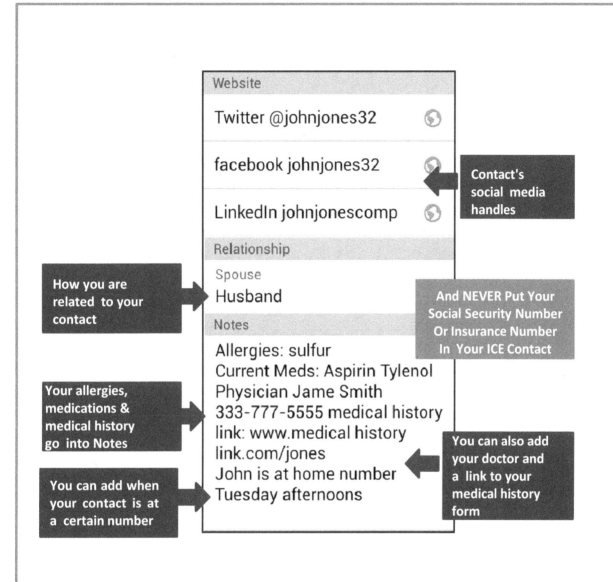

Website

Twitter @johnjones32

facebook johnjones32

LinkedIn johnjonescomp

Relationship

Spouse
Husband

Notes

Allergies: sulfur
Current Meds: Aspirin Tylenol
Physician Jame Smith
333-777-5555 medical history
link: www.medical history
link.com/jones
John is at home number
Tuesday afternoons

Contact's social media handles

And NEVER Put Your Social Security Number Or Insurance Number In Your ICE Contact

How you are related to your contact

Your allergies, medications & medical history go into Notes

You can add when your contact is at a certain number

You can also add your doctor and a link to your medical history form

How To Put Full ICE Contacts On Your Smartphones

During Hurricane Katrina and the London bombings, so many people were injured, unconscious and separated from their families that a British paramedic, Bob Brotchie came up with the idea of putting ICE Contacts (In Case Of Emergency) on cell phones. Now, when a patient who is unconscious or unable to speak comes into the emergency room, hospitals worldwide check patient's smartphones for an ICE contact, to help them locate their next of kin.

Everyone in your family should have an ICE contact in his or her smartphone. In fact, they should actually have two just in case the first contact is unavailable.   And even if you already have an ICE Contact, that doesn't mean that it has everything in it that it should, to save your life or the life of your spouse or your children.

If you already have an ICE Contact on your phone, don't just skip this section. Take a look at shortcut sheet to make sure your contact has everything it should, before using the instructions to ICE all the other phones in your household.

Since every type of smartphone is different, we have separate instructions on each type of phone.

Just go to the section for your type of phone and let's get started! You'll find instructions for Windows and Non Galaxy Android phones in the downloads.

iPhone & Apple Health ID

How To Put An ICE Contact On Your iPhone & Your Apple Medical ID

iPhones are always getting better and Apple's newest effort at keeping customers safe — Medical ID — is amazing. But as much as we LOVE it, there are two reasons you still need to make a regular ICE Contact.

1. You can put an unlimited amount of vital information into a regular contact.

2. Hospitals are used to looking for ICE Contacts rather than Medical ID and if you don't have a regular one, they might miss it.

And with the way the world has been the last few years — remember Hurricane Harvey, and Maria, the California wildfires not to mention COVID-19 — having an ICE contact is an awesome way keep your family safe and connected no matter WHAT is happening around you.

Here's what you'll need:

All of the contact info for your two (or more) emergency contacts.

- A list of your allergies.
- A list of your medical conditions/recent surgeries
- The contact information for your main physician(s)
- Any other information you would like an ER to know about you.

Grab your phone and let's get started!

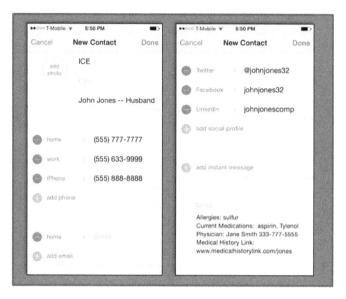

1. Put the word ICE, all capitals, in the First Name field. Don't type anything else in this field!

2. Put your ICE Contact's full name and relationship to you in the Company field, ie John Smith – Husband.

3. Type in every phone number you have for your contact.

4. Type in all of your contact's email addresses — again, every last one.

5. Type in all of your contact's social media handles/user names. You never know what will be up and running in an emergency. Many people have reached loved ones on Facebook and Twitter, when cell phone and landline service was down.

6. All of your own allergies, medications and medical history go in the notes section. Even better capitalize the words ALLERGIES, MEDICATIONS etc to ensure that they're seen.

7. Add your physician's names and phone numbers in the notes section and if you like, a link to your own Medical History Form. You'll find one in this book and in the downloads that came with it.

8. Is your contact in different locations on different days? Add that in the notes section.

9. Instead of their photo, add an ICE Contact Graphic to the contact to make it stand out. Go to the files you downloaded at the beginning of the book to find your favorite.

10. And finally, never put your social security number or insurance member number into your ICE Contact. You can add the name of your insurance company and customer service number, but the actual numbers can wait until later.

By the way, remember that you can fill in your ICE Contact on your Mac or iPad. Not only is it easier to type on a larger screen, but once you save it to your contacts, it will sync with iCloud and appear right on your phone.

And now, let's make your ICE info even easier to find, by setting up your iPhone's Medical ID.

What Is Medical ID?

Medical ID, a part of the Apple Health App, not only gives you a place to put your emergency medical information, but it puts a link to that information right on the front of your phone, where it can be viewed by a hospital even if your phone is password locked.

You'll find it on most iPhones (iPhone 6 and up) using iOS 8 and higher. If your phone is older and doesn't have Medical ID, you can just leave your ICE Contact the way it is.

On your home screen click on the Health App – it's the one with the heart on it. This will take you to the Dashboard page of the Health App. On the bottom right of the screen, you'll see the Medical ID icon. Click on it.

On the Medical ID screen, click on the red link that says Create Medical ID.

The most important part of the Medical ID screen is at the top. It's the On/Off Switch that shows a link to your emergency information on the home screen of your phone even when it's password-locked.

Before you do anything else, switch this to the ON position. It will turn green like the graphic below.

By the way, none of the information in your Medical ID is shared with any of the other apps on your phone.

Enter All Of Your Information

Put all the information you possibly can into your Medical ID.

As you can see it already has fields for your birth date, medical conditions, allergies, current medications and other information. There are two sections that you need to pay special attention to – Medical Notes and Add Emergency Contact.

After you finish filling in the regular fields, use the Notes Section to list anything that didn't fit into them, like the names and phone numbers of your physicians and healthcare providers and contact information for your Insurance Company. Again, don't add any sensitive personal information like a social security number, insurance member ID number or financial information.

You can also place a link to your Medical History Form in the Notes Section to give emergency personnel to quick access to your medical history until your emergency contact arrives at the hospital.

Add Your Emergency Contact

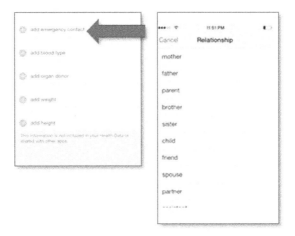

When you click on Medical ID's Add Emergency Contact button, it will show you a list of your contacts, so you can choose the people you'd like to add to your Medical ID. That's why we had you set up your ICE Contacts first.

Go ahead and click on the button and choose your first ICE Contact.

If you have additional ICE Contacts (a smart idea, in case your first contact is unreachable), then click on the Add Emergency Contact field again to add as many additional people as you would like.

Want to save time turning your husband or wife's contact into an ICE Contact? Simple! Just tap & hold the contact you want to use, choose share and email it to yourself. Then open it in your email, make the changes from above to turn it into an ICE Contact and save it to your contacts as ICE.

That's all there is to it!

And don't forget to put ICE Contacts on your spouse's and kid's phones too, along with each other's contact information, so you can all get in touch with each other quickly in an emergency.

Having an ICE contact and Medical ID is an awesome way keep your family safe and connected no matter WHAT is happening around you.

Samsung Galaxy Phone

GET YOUR
STUFF TOGETHER

**How To Set Up An ICE Contact
On Your Samsung Galaxy**

What is ICE?

During Hurricane Katrina, so many people were injured & separated from their families, that emergency workers came up with the idea of putting an ICE – In Case Of Emergency – contact in their cell phones. Now, hospitals worldwide, check patient's phones for their ICE contact, to locate their next of kin.

Everyone in your family should have 2 ICE contacts on his cell phone, just in case the first person is unavailable. So let's learn how to set up your ICE contact on your Samsung Galaxy.

Grab Your Phone & Let's Get Started 1

Who will your two ICE Contacts be? Your spouse, partner, best friend?

Once you decide, **Touch** the **Contacts Icon** on your Galaxy to open up your Contacts. Click on the plus sign **+** (or the 3 dots (...) then the +)**,** to add a new contact .

Then **touch the First Name Field.** Don't put the contact's name in this field, only the word **ICE,** because your Galaxy sorts contacts by their first name.

Next, touch the **Last Name Field** and enter your contact's full name, ie. John Jones.

When someone looks at the contact, they'll see ICE along with your emergency contact's full name. Do the same thing for your second ICE contact – just call it ICE2.

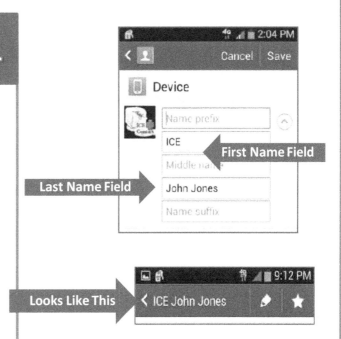

Enter All Of Your Information 2

Put **all the information you possibly can** into your two ICE Contacts. For example:

- Your emergency contact's **Main Number/Cell number/ Work number**, **Relationship** to you
- **Email Address & IM, Twitter and Facebook** address (in case landlines are down & you need to send an emergency message)
- Other info, for example, days that the contact is at a certain location
- Add **extra fields** if you need them.
- Use the **Notes Section** to list your Allergies, Current Medications or the Names & Numbers of your Physicians.

Notes Section →

Social Media →

← Relationship

Adding Fields 3

To add fields to your contact, press and hold the field name until the menu appears, then check the boxes next to the field/label you want and clicking OK.

One great field to add is **Relationship**, to tell emergency personnel who your contact is to you.

What About Your Medical History? 4

Need more than just a few lines to communicate your medical history? Then create a medical history form and store it to a password protected online folder & place a link to the form in your ICE contact.

This way a doctor can access your, your spouse's or your kids basic medical history, while you're en route to the hospital. You'll find your Medical Information Forms in the materials you downloaded at the beginning of the book and a Shortcut Sheet in the chapter on Medical History.

Make Your ICE Contacts Stand Out | 5

Make your ICE contacts stand out, by using the **Add Photo** function to upload a graphic to your phone, like the ones on this page.

You can make your own, or use ours. You'll find them with the Forms you downloaded at the beginning of the book. Save the graphic to the photos on your phone. Open your ICE Contact, **Touch** the little photo icon, **Choose Image**, pick the graphic you want and **Save**.

Touch Photo Icon & Choose Image

What If You Lock Your Phone? | 6

If you lock your phone with a password, it would be difficult for emergency personnel to retrieve your **ICE Contact**. But don't worry. There are 2 ways around that.

Most Samsung Galaxies have an **Emergency Dialer** on the **Home Screen**. Simply set up your ICE contacts and then press and hold your first ICE contact until the menu appears, then add it to the **ICE Emergency Contact Group**. Now it will appear on your emergency dialer.

What If You Don't Have Emergency Dialer?

If you lock your phone with a password, it's difficult for emergency personnel to retrieve your **ICE Contact**. But don't worry. All you have to do is add your ICE information directly to your **Lock Screen**.

Here's how you do it.

Go into **Settings** and touch **My Device** and then **Lock Screen**. Then touch **Lock Screen Widgets**. Now on the very bottom of the menu you'll see **Owner Information**. Touch that and a window will appear.

Simply type in "ICE CONTACT" along with your contact's name, phone number, your allergy or medical information – anything you would need an emergency room to know about you. Then **Check the Box** and Choose **Okay**.

Now your ICE information will appear right on your Lock Screen, no password needed.

Even though these directions for the Samsung Galaxy, most Android phones have this ability. Just look at your phone's manual to find out how to add text to your phone's lock screen.

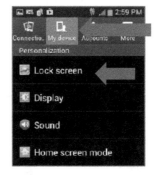

ICE Contact Appears On Lock Screen

Your Own Mobile Command Center

While you're at it, you can even **turn your phone** into a **Mobile Command Center**. Just store copies of your family's medical history forms, emergency action plans, checklists and Evacuation Plan (which you can find in our book Keep Everything You Love Safe, right on your phone and the phones of each member of your immediate family.

And don't forget to put ICE Contacts on their phones as well.

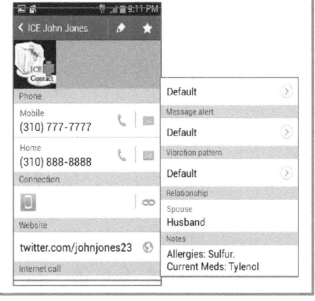

iPhone 4 & 5

What is ICE?

During Hurricane Katrina, so many people were injured & separated from their families, that emergency workers came up with the idea of putting an ICE – In Case Of Emergency – contact in their cell phones. Now, hospitals worldwide, check patient's phones for their ICE contact, to locate their next of kin. Everyone in your family should have 2 ICE contacts on his cell phone, just in case the first person is unavailable. So let's learn how to set up your ICE contact on your Android Smartphone..

Grab Your Phone & Let's Get Started

1

Who will your two ICE Contacts be? Your spouse, partner, best friend, parent or close relative?

Once you decide, **Touch** the **Contacts Icon** on your iPhone to open up your Contacts. Click on the plus sign **+** to add a new contact and **touch the Name Field**. Don't put the name of your contact in this field, only the word **ICE**.

Now touch the **Company Name Field**. This is where you put your contact's name and relationship to you. For example, John Jones - Husband.

Open Contacts

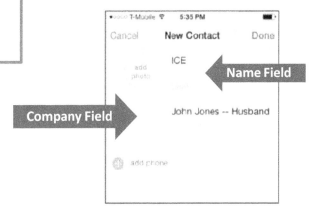

Name Field

Company Field

Enter All Of Your Information

2

Put **all the information you possibly can** into your two ICE Contacts. For example:

- Your emergency contact's Main Number/Cell number/ Work number
- Email Address & IM, Twitter and Facebook address (in case landlines are down & you need to send an emergency message)
- Other info, for example, days that the contact is at a certain location
- Add extra fields if you need them.
- Use the Notes Section to list your Allergies, Current Medications or the Names & Numbers of your Physicians.

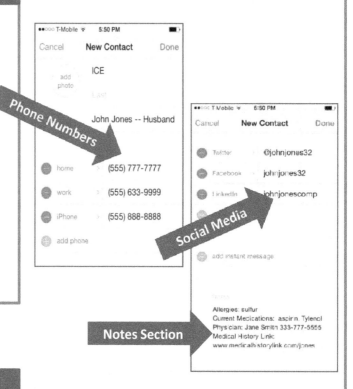

Phone Numbers

Social Media

Notes Section

What About Your Medical History?

3

Need more than just a few lines to communicate your medical history? Then create a medical history form and store it to a password protected online folder & place a link to the form in your ICE contact. This way a doctor can access your, your spouse's or your kids basic medical history, while you're en route to the hospital. You'll find your Medical Information Forms in the materials you downloaded at the beginning of the book and a Shortcut Sheet in the chapter on Medical History.

By the way, don't forget to make emergency cards for you and your family too. You'll find instructions later in this book.

To add fields to your contact, press the field name until the menu appears, then choose the field or label you want.

What About Your Medical History?

4

Need more than just a few lines to communicate your medical history? Then create a medical history form and store it to a password protected online folder & place a link to the form in your ICE contact.

This way a doctor can access your, your spouse's or your kids basic medical history, while you're en route to the hospital. You'll find your Medical Information Forms in the materials you downloaded at the beginning of the book and a Shortcut Sheet in the chapter on Medical History.

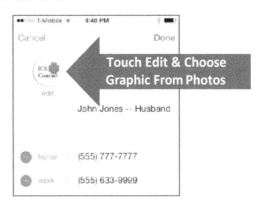

Touch Edit & Choose Graphic From Photos

What If You Lock Your Phone?

5

THAT's why we had you put nothing but the word ICE in the Name field of your ICE Contact. Even when your iPhone is password locked, all an Emergency Room has to do is **Press and Hold Down** the **Main Home Key** on your phone to access Siri.

Then say to Siri, "**Contacts ICE**". Siri will then display all the information you have saved as ICE. This won't work on some iPhones. It depends on the model and operating system.

To test your phone, set up your ICE contact, lock your iPhone and ask Siri to locate the contact . If it doesn't work, simply put your ICE Contact information on your lock screen as a graphic.

Problem solved!

Your Own Mobile Command Center

6

While you're at it, you can even **turn your phone** into a **Mobile Command Center**. Just store copies of your family's medical history forms, emergency action plans, checklists and Evacuation Plan (which you can find in our book **Keep Everything You Love Safe**), right on your phone and the phones of each member of your immediate family.

And don't forget to put ICE Contacts on their phones as well.

Completed Contact

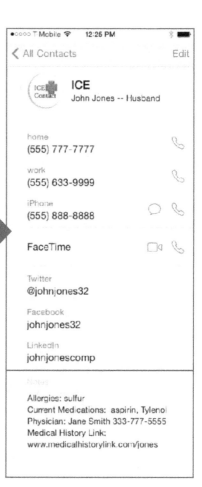

Android Phone

What is ICE?

During Hurricane Katrina, so many people were injured & separated from their families, that emergency workers came up with the idea of putting an ICE – In Case Of Emergency – contact in their cell phones. Now, hospitals worldwide, check patient's phones for their ICE contact, to locate their next of kin. Everyone in your family should have 2 ICE contacts on his cell phone, just in case the first person is unavailable. So let's learn how to set up your ICE contact on your Android Smartphone..

Grab Your Phone & Let's Get Started   1

Who will your two ICE Contacts be? Your spouse, partner, best friend, parent or close relative?

Once you decide, **Touch** the **Contacts Icon** on your phone to open up your Contacts. Click on the plus sign **+** to add a new contact and **touch the First Name Field.**

Don't put the name of your contact in this field, only the word **ICE.** This is because most phones sort contacts by their first name by default.

Next, touch the **Last Name Field** and enter your contact's full name and relationship to you, ie. John Jones Husband.

Now when someone looks at the contact, they'll see ICE along with your emergency contact's full name. Do the same thing for your second ICE contact – just call it ICE2.

Enter All Of Your Information 2

Put **all the information you possibly can** into your two ICE Contacts. For example:

- Your emergency contact's **Main Number/Cell number/ Work number**
- **Email Address & IM, Twitter and Facebook** address (in case landlines are down & you need to send an emergency message)
- Other info, for example, days that the contact is at
a certain location
- Add **extra fields** if you need them.
- Use the **Notes Section** to list your Allergies, Current Medications or the Names & Numbers of your Physicians.

Notes Section

Social Media

Numbers & Email

Adding Fields 3

To add fields to your contact, press and hold the **Field Name** or the "**Other**" Drop Down until the **Select Label** menu appears, then check the boxes next to the field/label you want and click OK.

One great field to add is **Relationship**, to tell emergency personnel who your contact is to you.

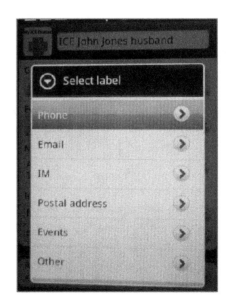

What About Your Medical History?

4

Need more than just a few lines to communicate your medical history? Then create a medical history form and store it to a password protected online folder & place a link to the form in your ICE contact. This way a doctor can access your, your spouse's or your kids basic medical history, while you're en route to the hospital. You'll find your Medical Information Forms in the materials you downloaded at the beginning of the book and a Shortcut Sheet in the chapter on Medical History.

By the way, don't forget to make emergency cards for you and your family too. You'll find instructions later in this book.

Creating A Communications Plan

5

Make your ICE contacts stand out, by using the **Add Photo** function to upload a graphic to your phone, like the ones on this page.

You can make your own, or use ours. You'll find them with the Forms you downloaded at the beginning of the book.

Save the graphic to the photos on your phone.

Open your ICE Contact, **Touch** the little photo icon, **Choose Gallery**, pick the graphic you want and **Save**.

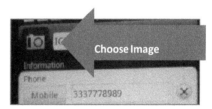

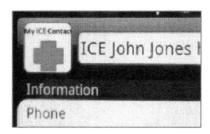

What If You Lock Your Phone?

If you lock your phone with a password, it's difficult for emergency personnel to retrieve your **ICE Contact**. But don't worry. All you have to do is add your ICE information directly to your **Lock Screen**.

Here's how you do it, using a Samsung Galaxy:

Go into **Settings** and touch **My Device** and then **Lock Screen**. Then touch **Lock Screen Widgets**. Now on the very bottom of the menu you'll see **Owner Information**. Touch that and a window will appear.

Simply type in "ICE CONTACT" along with your contact's name, phone number, your allergy or medical information – anything you would need an emergency room to know about you. Then **Check the Box** and Choose **Okay**.

Now your ICE information will appear right on your Lock Screen, no password needed.

Even though these directions for the Samsung Galaxy, most Android phones have this ability. Just look at your phone's manual to find out how to add text to your phone's lock screen.

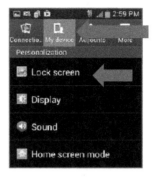

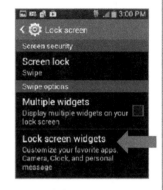

ICE Contact Appears On Lock Screen

Your Own Mobile Command Center

While you're at it, you can even **turn your phone** into a **Mobile Command Center**. Just store copies of your family's medical history forms, emergency action plans, checklists and Evacuation Plan (which you can find in our book **Keep Everything You Love Safe**), right on your phone and the phones of each member of your immediate family.

And don't forget to put ICE Contacts on their phones as well.

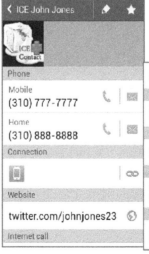

Windows Phone

What is ICE?

During Hurricane Katrina, so many people were injured & separated from their families, that emergency workers came up with the idea of putting an ICE – In Case Of Emergency – contact in their cell phones. Now, hospitals worldwide, check patient's phones for their ICE contact, to locate their next of kin. Everyone in your family should have 2 ICE contacts on his cell phone, just in case the first person is unavailable. So let's learn how to set up your ICE contact on your Nokia Lumia, HTC or other Windows Phone.

Grab Your Phone & Let's Get Started

1

Who will your two ICE Contacts be? Your spouse, partner, best friend, parent or close relative? Once you decide, **Tap on Start**, **Tap People**, Swipe over to **Contacts, Tap New** and if prompted, choose which account you want to add this contact to. **Touch Name**.

Type the word ICE first, followed by your contact's first and last name. Why do you want to do this? The Windows Phone sorts your contacts by first name, by default. So unless you have changed it to sort by last name, emergency personnel will see the word ICE right away.

Do the same thing for your second ICE contact – just call it ICE2.

Here's a tip: If your phone sorts by Last Name, you can change it by going into your **People Settings** and checking "Sort List By" First Name instead of Last Name.

Name

Enter All Of Your Information   2

Put **all the information you possibly can** into your two ICE Contacts. For example:

- Your emergency contact's **Main Number/Cell number/ Work number, Relationship** to you
- **Email Address, IM, Twitter and Facebook** address (in case landlines are down & you need to send an emergency message)
- Other necessary information, like the days that the contact is at a certain location

Adding Fields   3

To **Add** additional fields or information to your contact, **Tap Other**. Use the **Notes Section** to list your Allergies, Current Medications or the Names & Numbers of your Physicians.

What About Your Medical History?   4

Need more than just a few lines to communicate your medical history? First create a medical history form and store it to a password protected online folder. Then place a link to the form in your ICE contact. This way a doctor can access your, your spouse's or your kid's basic medical history, while you're en route to the hospital. You'll find your Medical Information Forms in the materials you downloaded at the beginning of the book and a Shortcut Sheet in the chapter on Medical History.

By the way, don't forget to make emergency cards for you and your family too. You'll find instructions later in this book.

18:59

EDIT GOOGLE CONTACT

other email

⊕ email

⊕ ringtone

⊕ text tone

home address

notes

Other →   ⊕ other

Make Your ICE Contacts Stand Out

5

Make your ICE contacts stand out, by using the **Add Photo** function to upload a graphic to your phone, like the ones on this page. You can make your own, or use ours. You'll find them with the Forms you downloaded at the beginning of the book.

Once you download the graphics to your desktop, **send** the one you'd like to use to your phone. Then open your ICE Contact, **Tap Add Photo**, choose the graphic you'd like and save it to your contact.

What If You Lock Your Phone?

6

If you normally lock your phone with a password, it might be difficult for emergency personnel to retrieve your **ICE Contact**. But don't worry. There is a way around that. All you have to do is add your ICE information directly to your **Lock Screen**. Here's how to do it in Windows Phone 8:

In the App list, **tap Settings** (looks like a gear) and choose **Lock Screen.** Expand the application bar on the bottom of the screen. Under Notifications, choose **Lock Screen Text** as the **app to show detailed status** and **touch** the back button.

Type "ICE Contact Information" in the text box, along with your contact's name, relationship and phone numbers. Fit in whatever you can. **Touch the check mark** to accept the change. If necessary, check **Done** to save your changes.

Now your ICE information will appear right on your Lock Screen, no password needed. Problem solved!

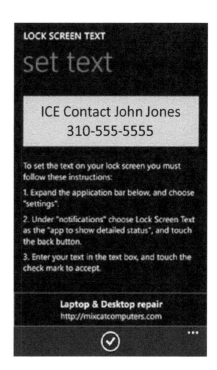

Your Own Mobile Command Center

While you're at it, you can even **turn your phone** into a **Mobile Command Center**. Just store copies of your family's medical history forms, emergency action plans, checklists and Evacuation Plan (which you can find in our book **Keep Everything You Love Safe**), right on your phone and the phones of each member of your immediate family.

And don't forget to put ICE Contacts on their phones as well.

Cell Phones That Aren't Smartphones

GET YOUR
STUFF TOGETHER

How To Set Up An ICE Contact On
A Non Smart Phone

What is ICE?

During Hurricane Katrina, so many people were injured & separated from their families, that emergency workers came up with the idea of putting an ICE – In Case Of Emergency – contact in their cell phones. Now, hospitals worldwide, check patient's phones for their ICE contact, to locate their next of kin. Everyone in your family should have 2 ICE contacts on his cell phone, just in case the first person is unavailable.

These instructions are for regular cell phones – not smartphones. But don't worry. Even if your phone isn't a smartphone, it's just as easy to set up an ICE Contact. Just keep in mind that every phone is different, so you might have to play around with the contact a bit, to get all the information you want to include.

Grab Your Phone & Let's Get Started   1

Who will your two ICE Contacts be? Your spouse, partner, best friend, parent or close relative? Once you decide, **Touch** the **Contacts Icon** on your phone to open up your Contacts.

Depending on the type of phone you have, your Contacts Icon might look different than the ones we have here. Click on **Add New** to add a new contact and **touch the First Name Field.** Don't put the name of your contact in this field, only the word **ICE.**

Next, touch the **Last Name Field** and enter your contact's full name and relationship to you, ie. John Jones Husband. Now when someone looks at the contact, they'll see ICE along with your emergency contact's full name. Do the same thing for your second ICE contact – just call it ICE2.

Contacts

Contacts

First Name

Last Name

Add New

Enter All Of Your Information

2

Put **all the information you possibly can** into your two ICE Contacts. For example:

- Your emergency contact's **Main Number/Cell number/ Work number**
- **Email Address & Social Media Contacts** like their **Facebook** address (in case landlines are down & emergency personnel need to send an emergency message)
- Other info, for example, days that the contact is at a certain location
- If you have a section for Notes in your contact, use the **Notes Section** to list your Allergies, Medications or Doctor's Contact Information.

Adding Fields

3

Need more than just a few lines to communicate your medical history? Then create a medical history form and store it to a password protected online folder & place a link to the form in your ICE contact. This way a doctor can access your, your spouse's or your kids basic medical history, while you're en-route to the hospital. You'll find your Medical Information Forms in the materials you downloaded at the beginning of the book and a Shortcut Sheet in the chapter on Medical History.

By the way, don't forget to make emergency cards for you and your family too. You'll find instructions later in this book.

What About Your Medical History?

4

Need more than just a few lines to communicate your medical history? Then create a medical history form and store it to a password protected online folder & place a link to the form in your ICE contact. This way a doctor can access your, your spouse's or your kids basic medical history, while you're en route to the hospital. You'll find your Medical Information Forms in the materials you downloaded at the beginning of the book and a Shortcut Sheet in the chapter on Medical History.

By the way, don't forget to make emergency cards for you and your family too. You'll find instructions later in this book.

Touch Photo Icon & Choose Image

Apple Watch

Did you ever wonder how to set up your Medical ID or ICE Contact on your Apple Watch?

As long as you have your iPhone handy, it couldn't be easier. One of the best things about the Apple Watch is that whatever information you put on your iPhone syncs up perfectly with your watch. Which is great news, when you're setting up your ICE Contact and Medical ID.

There's nothing worse than trying to type on a tiny little screen, right? If you've already set up your ICE Contacts and Medical ID on your iPhone, you're already set. All you or a hospital has to do is press and hold the side button on your watch.

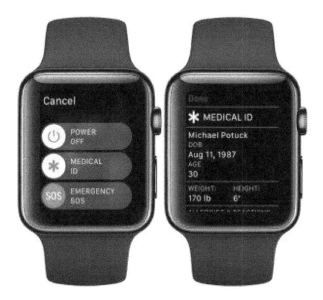

The Medical ID slide button will appear. Just tap it and you'll see your Medical ID information. Scroll down to emergency contacts, to view any ICE Contacts you added to the Medical ID on your iPhone.

If you happen to be a medical professional or a first responder, this is a great way to find an unconscious patient's medical and emergency information.

But what if you haven't set up your ICE Contacts and Medical ID on your iPhone yet? Not to worry! Here's how to do it the RIGHT way, in just a few minutes.

How To Set Up Your ICE Contacts and Medical ID On Your iPhone

As much as we love Apple's Medical ID, there are two reasons you still need to make a regular ICE Contact, to use along with it.

Number 1: You can put an unlimited amount of vital information into a regular contact.

Number 2: Hospitals are used to looking for ICE Contacts rather than Medical ID and if you don't have a regular one, they might miss it.
And with the way the world has been the last few years — remember Hurricane Harvey, Hurricane Irma, Maria and the California wildfires, not to mention Coronavirus — having an ICE contact is an awesome way keep your family safe and connected no matter WHAT is happening around you.

Below, you'll find everything you need not only to set up your Medical ID the RIGHT way, but the ICE Contacts that go along with it.

First grab the information you'll need:

All of the contact info for your two (or more) emergency contacts.

- A list of your allergies.
- A list of your medical conditions/recent surgeries
- The contact information for your main physician(s)
- Any other information you would like an ER to know about you.

Grab your phone and let's get started!

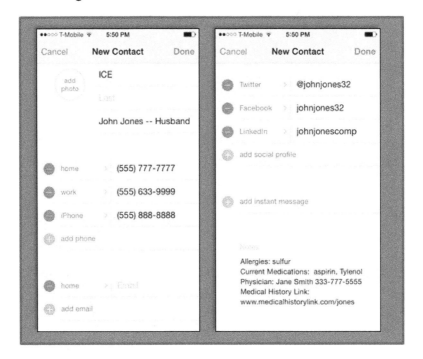

1. Put the word ICE, all capitals, in the First Name field. Don't type anything else in this field!

2. Put your ICE Contact's full name and relationship to you in the Company field, ie John Smith – Husband.

3. Type in every phone number you have for your contact.

4. Type in all of your contact's email addresses — again, every last one.

5. Type in all of your contact's social media handles/user names. You never know what will be up and running in an emergency. Many people have reached loved ones on Facebook and Twitter, when cell phone and landline service was down.

6. All of your own allergies, medications and medical history go in the notes section. Even better capitalize the words ALLERGIES, MEDICATIONS etc to ensure that they're seen.

7. Add your physician's names and phone numbers in the notes section and if you like, a link to your own Medical History Form. You'll find one right here in the book.

8. Is your contact in different locations on different days? Add that in the notes section as well.

9. Instead of their photo, add an ICE Contact Graphic to the contact to make it stand out. Go to our Free Resource Page to find one you love.

10. And finally, never put your social security number or insurance member number into your ICE Contact. You can add the name of your insurance company and customer service number, but the actual numbers can wait until later.

And now, let's make your ICE info even easier to find, by setting up your iPhone's Medical ID.

By the way, don't forget that you can fill in your ICE Contact on your Mac or iPad. Not only is it easier to type on a larger screen, but once you save it to your contacts, it will sync with iCloud and appear right on your phone.

What Is Medical ID?

Medical ID, a part of the Apple Health App, not only gives you a place to put your emergency medical information, but it puts a link to that information right on the front of your phone, where it can be viewed by a hospital even if your phone is password locked.

You'll find it on most iPhones (iPhone 6 and up) using iOS 8 and higher.   If your phone is older and doesn't have Medical ID, you can just leave your ICE Contact the way it is.

On your home screen click on the Health App – it's the one with the heart on it. This will take you to the Dashboard page of the Health App. On the bottom right of the screen, you'll see the Medical ID icon. Click on it.

On the Medical ID screen, click on the red link that says Create Medical ID.

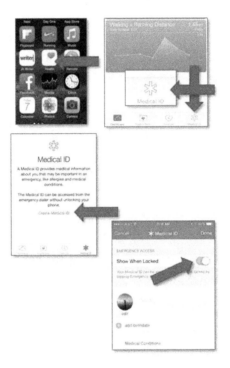

The most important part of the Medical ID screen is at the top. It's the On/Off Switch that shows a link to your emergency information on the home screen of your phone even when it's password-locked.

Before you do anything else, switch this to the ON position. It will turn green like the graphic below.

By the way, none of the information in your Medical ID is shared with any of the other apps on your phone.

Enter All Of Your Information

Put all the information you possibly can into your Medical ID.

As you can see it already has fields for your birth date, medical conditions, allergies, current medications and other information. There are two sections that you need to pay special attention to. Medical Notes and Add Emergency Contact.

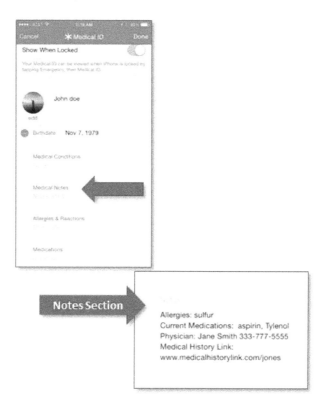

After you finish filling in the regular fields, use the Notes Section to list anything that didn't fit into them, like the names and phone numbers of your physicians and healthcare providers and contact information for your Insurance Company. Again, don't add any sensitive personal information like a social security number, insurance member ID number or financial information.

You can also place a link to your Medical History Form in the Notes Section to give emergency personnel to quick access to your medical history until your emergency contact arrives at the hospital.

Add Your Emergency Contact

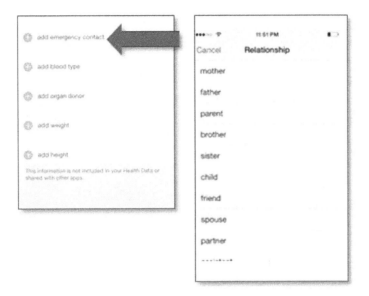

When you click on Medical ID's Add Emergency Contact button, it will show you a list of your contacts, so you can choose the people you'd like to add to your Medical ID. That's why we had you set up your ICE Contacts first.

Go ahead and click on the button and choose your first ICE Contact.

If you have additional ICE Contacts (a smart idea, in case your first contact is unreachable), then click on the Add Emergency Contact field again to add as many additional people as you would like.

Want to save time turning your husband or wife's contact into an ICE Contact? Simple! Just tap & hold the contact you want to use, choose share and email it to yourself. Then open it in your email, make the changes from above to turn it into an ICE Contact and save it to your contacts as ICE.

That's all there is to it!

Don't forget to put ICE Contacts on your spouse's and kid's phones too, along with each other's contact information, so you can get in touch with each other quickly and easily.

Having an ICE contact and Medical ID is an awesome way keep your family safe and connected no matter WHAT is happening around you.

The Smart Contact

Creating A Smart Contact

An ICE Contact can be a real lifesaver, especially in an emergency, when an ER doctor can use it to learn everything she needs to know about your medical history in one minute flat.

But thankfully life-threatening emergencies don't happen every day. What DOES happen, is that moms, dads and caregivers need to have important details about their children, their parents and the people they care for, at their fingertips.

Whether you're at the doctor, registering for school, visiting a specialist, or sitting in the emergency room with a slightly dented child, you never know when you're going to need potentially lifesaving details for the people you love.

That's why we re-engineered the entire concept of the ICE Contact, by turning it on its head.

Meet the Smart Contact – the contact that gives you all of the information you need, right in your smartphone. Not only will it come in handy in any of the situations we mentioned above, but it also contains all of the contact information you need to locate and gather your family members in minutes.

Simply create one Smart Contact for each member of your immediate family and if necessary, your parents and adult children. You probably already have a contact on your phone for many of these people, so simply add the information on the shortcut sheet below to their existing contact, to transform it into the perfect Smart Contact.

GET YOUR STUFF TOGETHER

Your Mission, Should You Choose To Accept It...

...is to set up a Smart Contact for each member of your immediate family, including your parents, adult children and any people for which you provide care. Since you already have a contact on your phone for most of these people, just add the information on the shortcut sheet below, to their contacts for an instant Smart Contact.

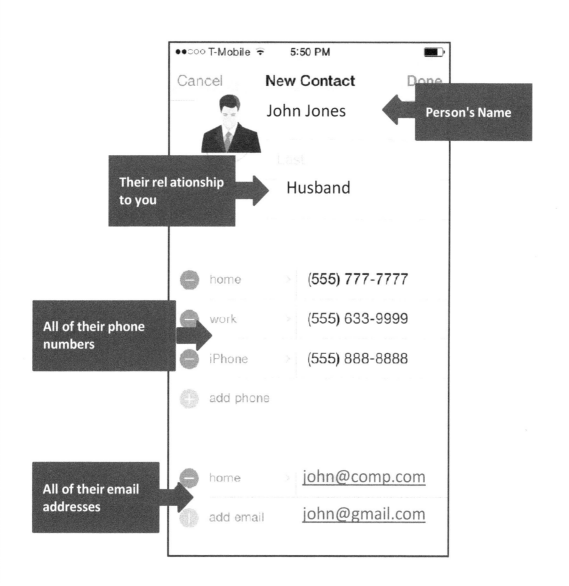

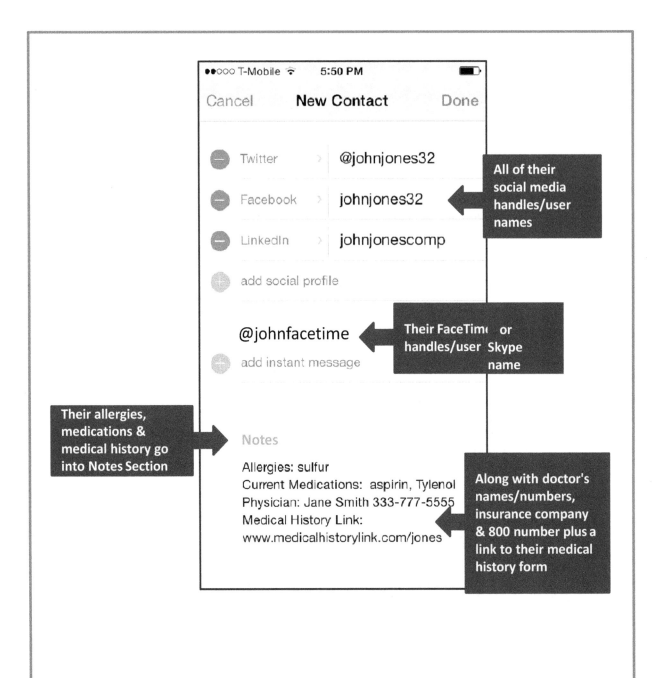

More Ways To Keep Yourself & Your Family Safe

It's All About Communication

This section is very personal to us, because we found out the hard way, how vital it can be to have this part of our lives absolutely organized, armor-plated, undefeatable and secure.

We'll never forget the day we realized it wasn't.

Elaine Sullivan was an active seventy-one year old living on her own in Chicago. One day while getting ready to take a bath, she slipped and fell, striking her head and mouth on the side of the tub. Her neighbors realized they hadn't seen her all day and called the paramedics, who went in and found her, conscious, but unable to speak.

She had previously been a patient at the hospital she was taken to, she had Medicare, supplemental insurance and everything she needed. Or so we thought. Even though she was stable, injuries to her mouth made her unable to speak or swallow, so she was unable to speak for herself. Over the next few days, after a series of serious medical errors and a critical drug interaction, her condition worsened.

Elaine Sullivan was my grandma.

Despite the fact that the hospital had my mother's and my contact information for our home in Los Angeles, the hospital neglected to call us for 6 1/2 days. By the time they did, Grandma was in critical condition from a lack of the most basic care. By the time we found out she'd been hospitalized, we were unable to get to her bedside before she died, unnecessarily and alone.

As we found out, hospitals don't always make calling your next of kin their priority. Even though hospitals try to find an unconscious patient's emergency contacts and notify their families in a reasonable amount of time, they can sometimes become so busy or are so understaffed that they don't make that call as quickly as they should.

We later found that one of the main factors that caused Grandma's death was the fact that the doctors treating her didn't have her medical or prescription drug history at their fingertips. If only they had called us, we could have given them that information. Of if she had had a cell phone back then, a simple ICE Contact in her phone detailing the prescription drugs she was taking, would have absolutely saved her life.

The moral of the story is that you never know what piece of information, no matter how small, might save the life of someone you love.

So are you ready to armor-plate your family? Then let's get started.

Medical Information

There's nothing worse than having something on the tip of your tongue and not being able to remember it – **except** when the word you're trying to remember is the name of a medication that the emergency room physician needs to save your daughter's life.

As everyone knows, when a patient is brought in the emergency room unconscious, aside from obvious injuries, the doctor caring for him probably has very little information about his patient. He has no idea what he might be allergic to, what medications he's taking or the surgery he had the month before.

Emergencies can rattle the best of us and the phone number or facts you know by heart are the very ones that will elude you when you need them most!

When it comes to you and your family, it's up to **you** to fill in that missing piece BEFORE emergencies happen. And you can't leave information that important, up to your memory.

Let's get it down on paper, where it belongs!

Your Mission, Should You Choose To Accept It...

...is to set up a Medical History Form for each member of your family. Open the Adult and Children's Medical History Forms (you'll find them with the forms you downloaded at the beginning of the book) and let's get started.

What Info Am I Going To Need? 1

Grab a pencil and paper and jot down the types of medical information you have for each member of the family. This includes your family's medical history, medical information, names of everyone's physicians, specialists, dentists, optometrists and other health care providers and current and past prescriptions.

Locate & Gather All Your Information 3

Using those notes and the list you completed in Step 1, **locate** and **gather** all of the medical information you have at home, along with your address book or contact information for physicians and the people you'll be using for emergency contacts.

What Do You Need A Doctor To Know? 2

Close your eyes for a moment & imagine that you're sitting in the ER with everyone in your house. One by one, imagine that your spouse, each child or your parent has an injury, like a broken arm, or needs emergency surgery. The doctor – who doesn't know you or your family's unique medical needs – walks through the door.

What does this doctor need to know about them? Jot down all of the things that just went through your mind. Old injuries, allergies, surgeries, anything you think is important.

Create Your Family's Medical History Forms 4

Grab the Medical Information Form you downloaded earlier and create one for each adult and child in your family, adding all of the information you've located.

Choosing Your Emergency Contacts 5

Choose and name at least 3 emergency contacts for each person, including yourself.
- Main Emergency Contact: Include your spouse on your form and yourself on your spouse's form. For your children - you &your spouse.
- 2nd Contact: A nearby relative or good friend who you would trust enough to make informed choices on your behalf, if necessary.
- 3rd Contact: should be an out of town/out of state relative or friend.

Anything Else To Add? 6

Is there any other information you need, to deal with a medical emergency while evacuated or away from home? If so, scan or make copies of that information and place it in the same folder as your completed medical history forms.

And while you're at it, don't forget to put ICE (In Case Of Emergency) Contacts in your and your family's smartphones along with a copy or link to your medical history forms. That way if you ever need quick access to a family member's medical history you'll have it right at your fingertips. Need instructions on ICE Contacts? Just go to that section of the book.

Now For Safekeeping... 7

Print, scan or make three copies of the form you just completed, along with the documents or other materials you need to have grabbable, and store them in at least **three** secure, damage-proof locations. That way if one or two of the locations are inaccessible, you'll still be able to grab the information you need.

You should also consider attaching the forms to your emergency contact cards (school & work) as well as placing a set on a secure web server and putting a link to them in your smartphone, so you'll always have your medical history forms at your fingertips wherever you are.

Your Emergency Wallet Cards

Think about your daily routine for a moment. Do you always take your phone and your wallet, purse or backpack with you when you go out? Or do you go running wearing nothing but a top, shorts, sneakers and an Air Pods? What about your spouse? Does he or she always carry a wallet and a phone, or almost never?

Do any of these "walletless" or "phoneless" situations sound familiar?
- The guy running out for a second with nothing but a few bucks to get a quart of milk.
- People out jogging, carrying nothing but some water and an iPod.
- The Alzheimer's patient who slips away from his caregiver and wanders down the street.
- The parents running out the door to pick up the kids, leaving their driver's license and other ID behind.
- The high-school or college students who don't "need" their student ID card to go out partying.

If you and your family don't have the information you need **with you w**hen you need it, all the emergency planning and information gathering you've done will do you absolutely no good!

Not to worry. We've got you covered – with Get Your Stuff Together's Emergency Wallet Cards. By the way, you can find them in the forms you downloaded at the beginning of this book. Just open them up on your computer, fill them out and print them, or print them out and fill them in by hand. You can even laminate them if you want.   Just be sure to create a card for every member of your immediate family.

Okay but what about those walletless situations? How will the wallet cards help me if I'm not carrying a wallet?

It's simple. Print out extra copies of the emergency wallet cards you'll be making and tuck them into the clothing or items that you take with you on your short jaunts.

Here's how to do it.

Your Mission, Should You Choose To Accept It...

...is to create an Emergency Wallet Card for each member of your family. These are great for situations when your you don't have a cell phone or regular wallet with you. Just slip them into a pocket, iPod, Shoewallet – any place.

Open The Wallet Card Document   1

Open up the Emergency Wallet Card from the forms and plans you downloaded at the beginning of the book. If you've been working through the other sections in the book, use the information and contacts you have gathered and Family Emergency/Evacuation Plans you have created to fill in a card for each member of your family.

The first side includes the person's name, birth year/blood type, physician and emergency contact names/numbers, allergies and if you want, a link to their medical information form. On the reverse are the details of your family's emergency plan.

Printing Out Your Wallet Cards   2

Once the cards are complete, print out wallet cards for each member of your family.

For the first set, print them out on thick cardstock – you can even laminate them – and place each one into a plastic lanyard (around the neck) card holder or a Shoewallet, and put them into your Plastic Evacuation Bin. Placing the wallet card into a card holder will not only keep it safe and dry, but will make it easy to locate and during an evacuation.

Where Else Can I Put Them?   3

Then print out two or three additional wallet cards for each person and place them in:
- Their regular wallets,
- Their work or school ID badges and
- Inside their Smartphone case
- One of several products, including our personal favorite the Shoewallet, that are tailor-made to hold your emergency wallet cards, along with your driver's license, credit cards, key and even a few dollars anytime you leave the house or the office without a purse or wallet. We happen to like Shoewallet because it securely fastens to your shoes, a belt loop, backpack or pocket.

When you stash emergency cards in different places, each member of your family will have a way to keep their emergency information and emergency plan available at all times, no matter where they are or what they're doing.

What About The Kids?   4

Since children don't carry wallets or driver's licenses, make sure that they have ID cards with current emergency contact information in a few different locations, like in a backpack, an inside jacket pocket, in a Shoewallet on their sneakers or tucked into the back of a cell phone or iPod.

How To Fill Out Your Family's Emergency Contact Cards

In the days after 9/11, 2,100 children were left stranded in daycare.

Why?

Because their parents neglected to fill out one field on their emergency contact cards.

"Who should we contact if you are not able to pick up your child?"

How could something so basic, strand two thousand children on one of the scariest days in American history?

Fear.

The inability or refusal to take two minutes to think through what might happen, if they and their spouse were unable to reach their child. The ridiculous thing is, it doesn't even have to take a real emergency for this to happen. You could be stuck on the freeway, or trapped in an airplane you were certain would arrive on time.

So take a few moments to think about it. And please, please don't just jot down the first name that pops into your head!

Imagine that you have an accident or are in the middle of a transportation nightmare and you and your spouse are unable to pick up your child from school one afternoon. Now imagine that you can't get to her for two or three days. Who would you want taking care of her?

Choosing Your Emergency Contacts

You need someone who knows your child extremely well. Someone who would be able to calm her down and would have the energy to care for her. Someone who knows what she likes and dislikes. And, in case of extreme emergency like September 11th, it would really help to have someone with the ability, brains and fortitude to help locate you or your spouse, if overburdened emergency personnel weren't able to help.

That's the kind of thought you need to put into emergency planning, especially where your children are concerned.

Medical History

Now what about your child's medical history? Some schools or day care centers don't even provide a card for medical history, or the one they provide might be so sparse that it would be useless in a true medical emergency. Don't forget that you can simply create your own medical history card and see that it's stored with your child's records. That way you can be sure that the information you would want emergency personnel to have in an emergency, will be right at their fingertips.

If you have already completed the section on Medical Information, you already have Medical History Forms for you and your children. So grab their forms and let's see how you did with them.

Did you include a current list of chronic conditions, allergies, medications and vitamins along with the dosage? A list of all of your child's health providers including specialists, dentists and other professionals who see your child on a regular basis?

Did you jot down things that a nurse or physician might need to know to help calm your child down while treating her, until you're able to be at the hospital? Your child's likes and dislikes, favorite foods or toys or anything else that might help. No matter how old your child is, kids tend to regress a bit when they're hurting or frightened, so the information you provide here can go a long way towards keeping them calm and helping the medical team give them the treatment they need until you arrive at the hospital.

Take the emergency contact card from your child's school or daycare provider and fill it in with your carefully-chosen emergency contacts as well as the information from the medical information form. Like we said, if there's not enough room to detail important information, just ask the school to store the medical information form you created earlier along with the emergency card. And be sure to store the medical information form, or a link to it, in your smartphone in case you need to refer to it in an emergency.

Your Own Emergency Contact Card

Just because you and your spouse are adults doesn't mean that you don't need to take your own emergency cards seriously. Do we have to remind you about all the runners who have been rushed to the hospital in the middle of a 10K without a scrap of medical information? Didn't think so!

The moment you begin a job, register for school or run a marathon, you're going to have to fill out your own card. The best way to do it? Exactly like you did for your kids.

Before you jot down your spouse and no one else as an emergency contact, take some time to think of another person or two, who you would want to be notified in an emergency. Your spouse might be out of town, stuck with a dead cell phone or worse might be involved in the same emergency.

If that's the case who would you want to be there with you? Who would you trust to make decisions for you? To take care of your children if need be, or keep things going until your spouse or other relatives arrive?

And take the same care with your medical history as you did with your children's. If there isn't enough room on the contact form for allergies, medications or other vital information, attach the medical information form you created earlier, or if you're not comfortable with that, attach an additional page of information to make sure your emergency form would actually help in an emergency!

Taking five minutes now to turn your emergency contact card into a truly valuable document, could be one of the smartest things you've ever done.

How To Make Your Family Findable

Living In A State of Constant Communication

In the middle of a busy, but quiet day in a Midwestern university lecture hall, the silence was pierced by a sudden hail of gunfire. Students ran out of the hall and ducked under tables. Those who couldn't move tried to make themselves as invisible as possible until help arrived. That day at Northern Illinois University, five students lost their lives. Many others were injured.

As the police and security were struggling to control the situation, a number of the student's parents not only knew that their children were all right, but they knew exactly what was happening in real time.

So how did some people have a window into the NIU tragedy while others did not? Facebook and Twitter! As unlikely as it sounds, students ingeniously found a way to use their favorite method of keeping in touch with friends, as a tool to connect to the outside world in the middle of a crisis.

Students caught under desks and tables grabbed their smartphones and started communicating. Tweets went out on Twitter, notes and messages went up on Facebook pages, telling friends and family that students, who were literally in the thick of things, were all right.

Others told loved ones or security officers the location of trapped students, facilitating their rescue. Friends started texting each other to find out where everyone was and, in the hours that followed, created Facebook pages memorializing the fallen.

It was an amazing display of people, who are connected 24/7, using that same technology to communicate, connect, survive and heal.

During the Japan earthquake cell phone towers barely worked because of earthquake damage and overloaded networks. But Wi-Fi was up and running. So what kept the Japanese connected with their families and the outside world? Twitter, Facebook, Skype and YouTube!

Smartphones, tablets and notebook computers are a phenomenal way to stay in touch during an emergency. Whether you send an email, text, tweet or Facebook message, you can find out the location and condition of everyone you love in seconds.   In a dire emergency, you can even send help, confirm or update emergency plans and even mobilize family and friends to be at the side of the ill or injured, using real time information.

Since disasters are completely unpredictable, the only way to prepare yourself and your family is to give yourselves as many different avenues of communication as possible. You never know which one will make the difference.

Want to learn how your family can use technology to communicate during an emergency? Then let's get started.

Your Mission, Should You Choose To Accept It...

...is to learn how your family can use technology to communicate during an emergency, then create a smartphone based communication plan to use the next time you have to gather everybody in a hurry.

Updating Your Smartphones 1

When you created your Family Evacuation Plan (if you haven't done that yet, go do it now – we'll wait for you), you listed the phone numbers, email addresses and social media addresses for each family member in your household.

Now we're going to take that one step further by adding all of that information to each family member's smartphones. While you're at it, add new contacts on everyone's phones for all of your out-of-area emergency contacts as well.

When Time Is An Issue 3

Using a social media platform like HootSuite.com may help. With HootSuite, you can send a single message that can be posted to Twitter, Facebook and LinkedIn simultaneously, ensuring that your family or friends would see your message immediately, no matter what site they happen to be on at the moment.

Direct Messaging 2

If cell phone service is down and you are unable to text, don't forget that Twitter and Facebook can also be used to send direct messages - personal messages that go only to the recipient . Here's a quick tutorial.

First, you need to make sure that every member of your family is following or has "liked" all of the other family members on Twitter and Facebook, so you can direct message each other.

- For Twitter, click on Messages, then Direct Messages and then type in @ and the family member's username. Then type in your message and hit send.
- For Facebook, click the little message icon at the top of your page (between the little people and the little bell). Then click Send New Message and type in the name of the recipient or recipients and click send.

The Value Of A Photo 4

During the Joplin tornado, even lifelong residents found themselves disoriented when the tornado turned their normal landmarks into kindling. If your spouse or kids don't know where they are after an emergency and need help a quick photo texted or uploaded to Instagram or Facebook could help you locate them. This is especially true of GPS enabled phones or photos with geo-location.

Creating A Communications Plan 5

Once you and your family have updated your phones and completed your evacuation plans, sit down with them to discuss the ways you can use technology to stay in touch with each other during a disaster.

Come up with some sample scenarios; for example, if a disaster were to happen while your family members were at work, at school or running errands during a normal day.

- How would you connect with each other?
- Would you text each other, or would calling or emailing be faster?
- If you have teens or young adults at home, their natural proclivity may be to send out a text or a tweet on Twitter, to update everyone, including you, on their location or situation.
- Find out the types of communication everyone prefers and then create an emergency communication plan that makes sense for your family.

Grab The Sat Phone! 7

If you're in an area with frequent emergencies like tornadoes or hurricanes, live out in the country or have a family member in a foreign country, consider getting satellite phones.

They work in remote areas where there is no cell phone coverage and when cell towers are down. Our favorite satellite phone provider is the BlueCosmo Inmarsat IsatPhone which provides you with global voice calling nearly any place on earth.

What If... 6

Another great discussion to have with your family, especially with school age children, is what they would do if they had to get a hold of you but the cell phone system was out, or what to do if there was an area-wide blackout. Don't laugh, that actually happed to us in California!

Kids are so used to technology that they might not have the experience that they need to do things the old school way. The best way to plan is to give yourselves as many ways as possible to stay connected. Then if one or two normal methods are unusable, you'll all simply turn to a different method to reach each other.

Code Word Clearance Or Higher 8

Consider creating a Family Emergency Code or Code Word. This is a code or word that only you and your immediate family know. When a family member says it, texts it or emails it to the rest of the family, it signals that they're in trouble and need help.

It's only to be used in extreme emergency and means that everyone needs to drop what they're doing and establish contact with each other, immediately.

Find My Family ASAP! 9

Find My Friends is an iPhone app that is designed to let you know at a glance where your friends are. But you can also use it to immediately locate your children, spouse and loved ones in an emergency.

All your family has to do is allow you access on their phones, and if need be, you can immediately see where everyone is in real time, complete with map and directions.

Get Your Stuff Together
Medical Information Forms and Emergency Wallet Cards

Section One	**Adult One Information**			
First Name	MI	Last Name	M/F	DOB
Religion	Home Phone	Cell Phone	Work Phone	Email Address
Address		City	State	Zip
Height/Weight	Blood Type	RH	Identifying Marks	

Section Two	**Emergency Contacts**					
Main Contact:						
First Name	Last Name		Relationship	Home Phone	Work Phone	Cell
Best Place to Reach Contact? Any Schedule Considerations? Notes?						

Contact Two						
First Name	Last Name		Relationship	Home Phone	Work Phone	Cell
Best Place to Reach Contact? Any Schedule Considerations? Notes?						

Contact Three						
First Name	Last Name		Relationship	Home Phone	Work Phone	Cell
Best Place to Reach Contact? Any Schedule Considerations? Notes?						

Work				
Employer	Title	Phone	Manager	
Address	City	State	Zip	

Section Three	**Medical Information**			
Primary Physician	Specialty	Phone	Alt Phone/Email	Hospital
Physician Two	Specialty	Phone	Alt Phone/Email	Hospital
Physician Three	Specialty	Phone	Alt Phone/Email	Hospital

Dentist	Specialty	Phone	Alt Phone/Email	Notes

Dentist Two	Specialty	Phone	Alt Phone/Email	Notes

Optometrist	Glasses/Contacts?	Phone	Alt Phone/Email	Location

Section Four	Prescription, Allergy & Chronic Condition Information

Prescription Information

Prescription Name	Dosage	Frequency	For what condition

Prescription Name	Dosage	Frequency	For what condition

Prescription Name	Dosage	Frequency	For what condition

Prescription Name	Dosage	Frequency	For what condition

Name of Pharmacy	Phone	Pharmacist	Location

Allergy Information

Allergy Type	Severity	Frequency/Last Occurrence/Notes

Allergy Type	Severity	Frequency/Last Occurrence/Notes

Allergy Type	Severity	Frequency/Last Occurrence/Notes

Chronic Conditions

Condition	Severity	Current Treatment/Notes

Condition	Severity	Current Treatment/Notes

Condition	Severity	Current Treatment/Notes

Immunizations

Immunization	Date	Immunization	Date

Immunization	Date	Immunization	Date

Immunization	Date	Immunization	Date

Section Five	Health Insurance

Insurance Company	Member Number	Group/Policy Number	Customer Service

Member Hospital	Agent Name	Agent Number	Notes
Insurance Company	Member Number	Group/Policy Number	Customer Service
Member Hospital	Agent Name	Agent Number	Notes

Section Six — Do You Have A....

Will?	Location	Power of Attorney?	Location
Living Will/Trust?	Location	Other	Location

Section Seven — Important Things To Know

Things I want an emergency physician to know about me

Things I want an emergency physician to know about my medical history

Any other notes, important numbers or wishes that need to be communicated

Section Eight — Recent Medical Procedures and Tests

Procedure 1	Date	Reason for Procedure
Physician	Hospital	Results
Procedure 2	Date	Reason for Procedure
Physician	Hospital	Results
Medical Test 1	Date	Reason for Procedure
Physician	Hospital	Results
Medical Test 2	Date	Reason for Procedure
Physician	Hospital	Results
Medical Test 3	Date	Reason for Procedure
Physician	Hospital	Results

Section Nine		Alternative Medicines and Other Substances Commonly Used	
Vitamins or Herbs Taken	Dosage	Frequency/Last Occurrence/Notes	
Vitamins or Herbs Taken	Dosage	Frequency/Last Occurrence/Notes	
Vitamins or Herbs Taken	Dosage	Frequency/Last Occurrence/Notes	
Substances or Alcohol Used	Frequency	Substances or Alcohol Used	Frequency
Substances or Alcohol Used	Frequency	Substances or Alcohol Used	Frequency
Substances or Alcohol Used	Frequency	Substances or Alcohol Used	Frequency

Section Ten		Counselors or Other Health Providers	
Counselor 1	Specialty	Phone	Alternate Phone
Counselor 2	Specialty	Phone	Alternate Phone

Adult Two - Medical

Section One	**Adult One Information**			
First Name	MI	Last Name	M/F	DOB
Religion	Home Phone	Cell Phone	Work Phone	Email Address
Address		City	State	Zip
Height/Weight	Blood Type	RH	Identifying Marks	

Section Two   **Emergency Contacts**

Main Contact:

First Name	Last Name	Relationship	Home Phone	Work Phone	Cell

Best Place to Reach Contact? Any Schedule Considerations? Notes?

Contact Two

First Name	Last Name	Relationship	Home Phone	Work Phone	Cell

Best Place to Reach Contact? Any Schedule Considerations? Notes?

Contact Three

First Name	Last Name	Relationship	Home Phone	Work Phone	Cell

Best Place to Reach Contact? Any Schedule Considerations? Notes?

Work

Employer	Title	Phone	Manager
Address	City	State	Zip

Section Three	**Medical Information**			
Primary Physician	Specialty	Phone	Alt Phone/Email	Hospital
Physician Two	Specialty	Phone	Alt Phone/Email	Hospital
Physician Three	Specialty	Phone	Alt Phone/Email	Hospital

Dentist	Specialty	Phone	Alt Phone/Email	Notes

Dentist Two	Specialty	Phone	Alt Phone/Email	Notes

Optometrist	Glasses/Contacts?	Phone	Alt Phone/Email	Location

Section Four — Prescription, Allergy & Chronic Condition Information
Prescription Information

Prescription Name	Dosage	Frequency	For what condition

Prescription Name	Dosage	Frequency	For what condition

Prescription Name	Dosage	Frequency	For what condition

Prescription Name	Dosage	Frequency	For what condition

Name of Pharmacy	Phone	Pharmacist	Location

Allergy Information

Allergy Type	Severity	Frequency/Last Occurrence/Notes

Allergy Type	Severity	Frequency/Last Occurrence/Notes

Allergy Type	Severity	Frequency/Last Occurrence/Notes

Chronic Conditions

Condition	Severity	Current Treatment/Notes

Condition	Severity	Current Treatment/Notes

Condition	Severity	Current Treatment/Notes

Immunizations

Immunization	Date	Immunization	Date

Immunization	Date	Immunization	Date

Immunization	Date	Immunization	Date

Section Five — Health Insurance

Insurance Company	Member Number	Group/Policy Number	Customer Service

Member Hospital	Agent Name	Agent Number	Notes

Insurance Company	Member Number	Group/Policy Number	Customer Service

Member Hospital	Agent Name	Agent Number	Notes

Section Six — Do You Have A....

Will?	Location	Power of Attorney?	Location

Living Will/Trust?	Location	Other	Location

Section Seven — Important Things To Know

Things I want an emergency physician to know about me

Things I want an emergency physician to know about my medical history

Any other notes, important numbers or wishes that need to be communicated

Section Eight — Recent Medical Procedures and Tests

Procedure 1	Date	Reason for Procedure
Physician	Hospital	Results
Procedure 2	Date	Reason for Procedure
Physician	Hospital	Results
Medical Test 1	Date	Reason for Procedure
Physician	Hospital	Results
Medical Test 2	Date	Reason for Procedure
Physician	Hospital	Results
Medical Test 3	Date	Reason for Procedure
Physician	Hospital	Results

Section Nine		Alternative Medicines and Other Substances Commonly Used		
Vitamins or Herbs Taken		Dosage	Frequency/Last Occurrence/Notes	
Vitamins or Herbs Taken		Dosage	Frequency/Last Occurrence/Notes	
Vitamins or Herbs Taken		Dosage	Frequency/Last Occurrence/Notes	
Substances or Alcohol Used	Frequency	Substances or Alcohol Used		Frequency
Substances or Alcohol Used	Frequency	Substances or Alcohol Used		Frequency
Substances or Alcohol Used	Frequency	Substances or Alcohol Used		Frequency
Section Ten		Counselors or Other Health Providers		
Counselor 1	Specialty		Phone	Alternate Phone
Counselor 2	Specialty		Phone	Alternate Phone

Section One — Child One Information

First Name	MI	Last Name	M/F	DOB

Religion	Home Phone	Cell Phone	Notes	

Address	City	State	Zip

Height/Weight	Blood Type	RH	Identifying Marks

Section Two — Emergency Contacts

Parent/Guardian One:

First Name	Last Name	Relationship	Home Phone	Work Phone	Cell Phone

Best Place to Reach Contact? Any Schedule Considerations? Notes?

Parent/Guardian Two:

First Name	Last Name	Relationship	Home Phone	Work Phone	Cell Phone

Best Place to Reach Contact? Any Schedule Considerations? Notes?

Contact Three

First Name	Last Name	Relationship	Home Phone	Work Phone	Cell Phone

Best Place to Reach Contact? Any Schedule Considerations? Notes?

School

School	Phone	Teacher	Grade

Address	City	Notes	

Babysitter	Phone	Afterschool Program #	Phone

Section Three		Medical Information		
Primary Pediatrician	Specialty	Phone	Alt Phone/Email	Hospital
Physician Two	Specialty	Phone	Alt Phone/Email	Hospital
Dentist	Specialty	Phone	Alt Phone/Email	Notes
Optometrist	Glasses/Contacts?	Phone	Alt Phone/Email	Location

Section Four	Prescription, Allergy & Chronic Condition Information		

Prescription Information

Prescription Name	Dosage	Frequency	For what condition
Prescription Name	Dosage	Frequency	For what condition
Prescription Name	Dosage	Frequency	For what condition
Prescription Name	Dosage	Frequency	For what condition
Name of Pharmacy	Phone	Pharmacist	Location

Allergy Information

Allergy Type	Severity	Frequency/Last Occurrence/Notes
Allergy Type	Severity	Frequency/Last Occurrence/Notes
Allergy Type	Severity	Frequency/Last Occurrence/Notes

Chronic Conditions

Condition	Severity	Current Treatment/Notes
Condition	Severity	Current Treatment/Notes

Immunizations

Immunization	Date	Immunization	Date
Immunization	Date	Immunization	Date
Immunization	Date	Immunization	Date

Section Five		Health Insurance		
Insurance Company	Member Number	Group/Policy Number	Customer Service
Member Hospital	Agent Name	Agent Number	Notes
Insurance Company	Member Number	Group/Policy Number	Customer Service
Member Hospital	Agent Name	Agent Number	Notes

Section Six	What I want an Emergency Physician to Know About My Child

What you need to know about my Child's Medical History

What you need to know about my Child's Personality

These are my Child's Likes and Dislikes

What Calms Her or Him Down

These are my child's Food Preferences and Bedtime Routines

Anything else I want you to know about my child

Section Seven	Recent Medical Procedures and Tests	
Procedure 1	Date	Reason for Procedure
Physician	Hospital	Results
Procedure 2	Date	Reason for Procedure
Physician	Hospital	Results
Medical Test 1	Date	Reason for Procedure
Physician	Hospital	Results
Medical Test 2	Date	Reason for Procedure
Physician	Hospital	Results

Section Eight	Alternative Medicines and Other Substances Commonly Used	
Vitamins or Herbs Taken	Dosage	Frequency/Last Occurrence/Notes
Vitamins or Herbs Taken	Dosage	Frequency/Last Occurrence/Notes
Vitamins or Herbs Taken	Dosage	Frequency/Last Occurrence/Notes

Section Nine	Counselors or Other Health Providers		
Counselor 1	Specialty	Phone	Alternate Phone
Counselor 2	Specialty	Phone	Alternate Phone

Card 1 (top-left)

Notes:

Alternate Meeting Place:

IM/Twitter:

Out of Town Contact:

Contact Name/#

Meeting Place:

Family Emergency Plan

GET YOUR STUFF TOGETHER Grab it and Go Emergency Card

Name:

Birth Yr/Blood Type:

Physician:

Contact:

Contact:

Allergies:

See ICE info in: My Cell phone

Card 2 (top-right)

Notes:

Alternate Meeting Place:

IM/Twitter:

Out of Town Contact:

Contact Name/#

Meeting Place:

Family Emergency Plan

GET YOUR STUFF TOGETHER Grab it and Go Emergency Card

Name:

Birth Yr/Blood Type:

Physician:

Contact:

Contact:

Allergies:

See ICE info in: My Cell phone

FOLD HERE

Card 3 (bottom-left)

Notes:

Alternate Meeting Place:

IM/Twitter:

Out of Town Contact:

Contact Name/#

Meeting Place:

Family Emergency Plan

GET YOUR STUFF TOGETHER Grab it and Go Emergency Card

Name:

Birth Yr/Blood Type:

Physician:

Contact:

Contact:

Allergies:

See ICE info in: My Cell phone

Card 4 (bottom-right)

Notes:

Alternate Meeting Place:

IM/Twitter:

Out of Town Contact:

Contact Name/#

Meeting Place:

Family Emergency Plan

GET YOUR STUFF TOGETHER Grab it and Go Emergency Card

Name:

Birth Yr/Blood Type:

Physician:

Contact:

Contact:

Allergies:

See ICE info in: My Cell phone

FOLD HERE

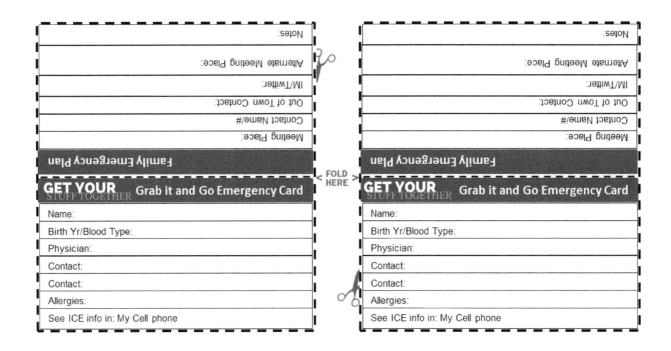

You can find all of our books – both paperback and instant PDF downloads – on the Books tab of our website www.getyourstufftogether.com.

Get Our Books At Bulk Rates For Your Business, Church, Service Club or Organization!
Email Us Through The Website For Details.

MEET THE
WHOLE FAMILY

A percentage of each product sold will go towards putting our newest book *#Alone Together*, into the hands of the families who need it. The book's mission? To help keep hospitalized COVID-19 patients from dying alone, by giving their families the tools they need to stay connected with them and their medical team.

To purchase masks, mugs & tee shirts   https://www.bonfire.com/store/getyourstufftogether/
To purchase phone cases   https://www.zazzle.com/s/wealthoftulips+phone+cases

Richly Red Smile Mask

Creativi-Tea Coffee &Tea Mug

Prosperi-Tee Tee Shirt

Pretty In Pink Smile Mask

Leftea Coffee &Tea Mug

Creativi-Tee Tee Shirt

Red Parrot Tulip Phone Case

Personali-Tee Tee Shirt

Tulips In Breeze Phone Case

GET YOUR STUFF TOGETHER MERCHANDISE

About The Authors

Janet and Laura are one of the only mother/daughter writing teams in the entertainment industry. They began their careers in production on network sitcoms at MGM and Warner Bros and are currently developing their own original movies and television series.

The Greenwalds were introduced to emergency preparedness the hard way, when a jumbo-jet crashed across the street from their home. But it was a horrendous medical tragedy – one that took the life of their mother/grandmother, Elaine Sullivan – that propelled them into new territory.

When Elaine's hospital failed to notify Jan and Laura of her hospitalization they were not only prevented from being at her side, but they were also kept from preventing the drug interaction that took Elaine's life.

After uncovering a loophole in the laws which regulate the notification of the next of kin of hospital patients, Laura & Jan joined forces with legislators in Illinois and California to enact three Next of Kin Laws, before creating Notify In 7, a training program that provides hospital professionals with the skills they need to notify and reunite trauma victims with their loved ones, quickly and easily. Hoping to keep other families from experiencing the same thing they had, they turned their story into a screenplay called Without Consent, now in development as a feature film.

Their book *Keep Everything You Love Safe*, gives readers quick and easy steps they can take to keep everything that's important to them organized, safe and accessible. Each section – over 30 in all – covers a different area from backing up & fixing family photos, home movies and music, to creating an evacuation plan, securing vital documents, medical information, financial information and data.

Between their books, blog and website, over 1.5 million people have used Jan and Laura's shortcut sheets, action plans and materials to keep themselves, their homes, their families and the things that they love, safe and secure.

www.ingramcontent.com/pod-product-compliance
Lightning Source LLC
LaVergne TN
LVHW080101070326
832902LV00014B/2355